Snap, snap

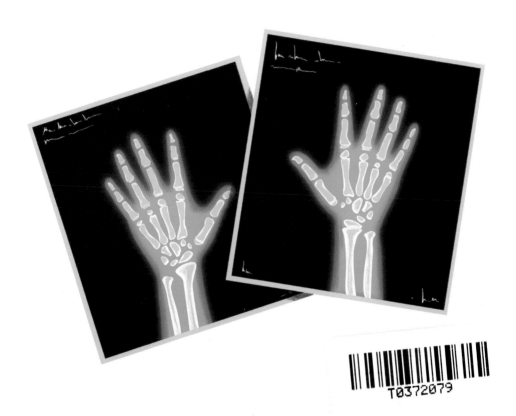

Dear Granny,
I have broken my wrists.
I asked Mum not to tell
you. I wanted to write to
you myself.

Now my arms aren't so
sore. But it will take me
a long time to write. I keep
typing the wrong letters!

I was playing ball at Ben's
and I fell hard onto my hands.
It hurt like mad. Then I felt sick.

Ben's dad put me in the car.
Ben came with us too.

The next thing, there were
nurses and a doctor. The
doctor gave me something
to make me feel a bit better
while they looked at my arms.

They put me in a wheelchair and off we went.

I had to get an X-ray. This let the doctor look inside to see what was wrong. By now my wrists looked bigger!

They saw that my wrists were
broken. But with all the little
bones in there, I could not tell.

I was feeling a bit better by then. Ben's dad told him off for pushing me too quickly to the lift but it was fun.

In another room a nurse
wrapped up my hands,
wrists and arms.

She put white stuff on them.
It dried quickly, then she
put covers on them. I chose
nice blue ones.

I have to keep my arms dry.
It's hard but Mum wraps
them up for me.

14

It is hard to get out of my clothes. My room is a wreck!

Now I have writing all
over my wrists! See
you soon, love Meg!

Words to blend

wrists	write	wrong
wrapped	wraps	writing
wreck	feeling	quickly
pushing	typing	wheelchair
covers	another	Granny
nurses	X-ray	room

Before reading

Synopsis: Meg tells Granny about her visit to the hospital to get treatment for her broken wrists.

Review phonemes and graphemes: /ear/ ere, eer; /air/ are, ear, ere; /j/ ge, dge, g; /s/ c, ce, sc, se, st; /c/ ch; /u/ o, o-e, ou; /e/ ea

Focus phoneme: /r/ **Focus grapheme:** wr

Story discussion: Look at the cover, and read the title together. Ask: *What do you think has happened to this girl? What do you think will happen in this book?* Look at the illustration on the title page. Ask: *Have you seen pictures like this before? What do they tell us?*

Link to prior learning: Remind children that the sound /r/ as in 'rub' can also be spelled 'wr'. Turn to pages 2–3 and ask children to find as many words with this spelling of the /r/ sound as they can (wrists, write, wrong).

Vocabulary check: X-ray: a way for doctors to take a picture of the inside of our bodies. Practise reading this word.

Decoding practice: Display the words 'writing', 'wrong', 'wreck' and 'wrists'. Can children circle the letter string that makes the /r/ sound, and read each word?

Tricky word practice: Display the word 'asked'. This word is only tricky in some accents – if the children pronounce it with a short /a/, don't teach it as tricky. Otherwise, remind children that the tricky part of this word is 'a', which says /ar/. Practise reading and spelling this word.

After reading

Apply learning: Discuss the book. Ask: *Have you ever been to the hospital or the doctors? If so, what was it like? What do you think about Meg's hospital visit?*

Comprehension

- How do you think Meg felt when she broke her wrists? What interesting words can you use? (shocked, upset, scared, etc.)
- How did Meg, Ben and Ben's dad get to the hospital? (Ben's dad drove them)
- How did the doctor know Meg had broken her wrists? (the X-ray showed the breaks)

Fluency

- Pick a page that most of the group read quite easily. Ask them to reread it with pace and expression. Model how to do this if necessary.
- Challenge children to read pages 4–5 as if they were talking to someone they know.
- Practise reading the words on page 17.

Tricky words review

have	asked	to
wanted	the	today
were	laugh	what
little	was	ones
of	because	friend